WONDER WOMAN™

MAD LIBS®

by Brandon T. Snider

Mad Libs
An Imprint of Penguin Random House

MAD LIBS
Penguin Young Readers Group
An Imprint of Penguin Random House LLC

Published by Mad Libs,
an imprint of Penguin Random House LLC,
345 Hudson Street, New York, New York 10014.
Printed in the USA.

ISBN 9781524788148
1 3 5 7 9 10 8 6 4 2

MAD LIBS® is a game for people who don't like games! It can be played by one, two, three, four, or forty.

• RIDICULOUSLY SIMPLE DIRECTIONS

In this tablet you will find stories containing blank spaces where words are left out. One player, the READER, selects one of these stories. The READER does not tell anyone what the story is about. Instead, he/she asks the other players, the WRITERS, to give him/her words. These words are used to fill in the blank spaces in the story.

• TO PLAY

The READER asks each WRITER in turn to call out a word—an adjective or a noun or whatever the space calls for—and uses them to fill in the blank spaces in the story. The result is a MAD LIBS® game.

When the READER then reads the completed MAD LIBS® game to the other players, they will discover that they have written a story that is fantastic, screamingly funny, shocking, silly, crazy, or just plain dumb—depending upon which words each WRITER called out.

• EXAMPLE (*Before* and *After*)

" _____ !" he said _____
    EXCLAMATION   ADVERB

as he jumped into his convertible _____ and
                                NOUN

drove off with his _____ wife.
                ADJECTIVE

" **OUCH** !" he said **STUPIDLY**
    EXCLAMATION   ADVERB

as he jumped into his convertible **CAT** and
                                NOUN

drove off with his **BRAVE** wife.
                ADJECTIVE

QUICK REVIEW

In case you have forgotten what adjectives, adverbs, nouns, and verbs are, here is a quick review:

An ADJECTIVE describes something or somebody. *Lumpy*, *soft*, *ugly*, *messy*, and *short* are adjectives.

An ADVERB tells how something is done. It modifies a verb and usually ends in "ly." *Modestly*, *stupidly*, *greedily*, and *carefully* are adverbs.

A NOUN is the name of a person, place, or thing. *Sidewalk*, *umbrella*, *bridle*, *bathtub*, and *nose* are nouns.

A VERB is an action word. *Run*, *pitch*, *jump*, and *swim* are verbs. Put the verbs in past tense if the directions say PAST TENSE. *Ran*, *pitched*, *jumped*, and *swam* are verbs in the past tense.

When we ask for A PLACE, we mean any sort of place: a country or city (*Spain*, *Cleveland*) or a room (*bathroom*, *kitchen*).

An EXCLAMATION or SILLY WORD is any sort of funny sound, gasp, grunt, or outcry, like *Wow!*, *Ouch!*, *Whomp!*, *Ick!*, and *Gadzooks!*

When we ask for specific words, like a NUMBER, a COLOR, an ANIMAL, or a PART OF THE BODY, we mean a word that is one of those things, like *seven*, *blue*, *horse*, or *head*.

When we ask for a PLURAL, it means more than one. For example, *cat* pluralized is *cats*.

MAD LIBS® is fun to play with friends, but you can also play it by yourself! To begin with, DO NOT look at the story on the page below. Fill in the blanks on this page with the words called for. Then, using the words you have selected, fill in the blank spaces in the story.

Now you've created your own hilarious MAD LIBS® game!

ORIGIN

ADJECTIVE _____

ADJECTIVE _____

PLURAL NOUN _____

NOUN _____

NOUN _____

VERB _____

PLURAL NOUN _____

FIRST NAME (FEMALE) _____

ADJECTIVE _____

ANIMAL _____

NOUN _____

A PLACE _____

A PLACE _____

NOUN _____

MAD LIBS®

A PRINCESS DREAMS

Life can be boring on _____ Island. That's what some of the
_____ADJECTIVE

other Amazons call our _____. Sure, there are _____
_____NOUN_____ADJECTIVE

waterfalls and _____ hills filled with _____,
_____COLOR_____ANIMAL (PLURAL)

but I want to see the rest of the world! Some days all I do is

_____ out my window. When I'm not _____ in
_____VERB_____VERB ENDING IN "ING"

(the) _____, that is. I wish I could hop on a/an _____ and
_____A PLACE_____NOUN

_____ away. That would be wonderful! My _____
_____VERB_____NOUN

won't let me use any of the _____ just yet. She says I'm too
_____PLURAL NOUN

young, but I'm _____ quickly, and soon I'll be
_____VERB ENDING IN "ING"

_____ years old. Mother tells me I have a/an _____
___NUMBER_____ADJECTIVE

_____. She says I'm destined to be like _____—
_____NOUN_____CELEBRITY

sharp and strong. I certainly hope she's right!

MAD LIBS® is fun to play with friends, but you can also play it by yourself! To begin with, DO NOT look at the story on the page below. Fill in the blanks on this page with the words called for. Then, using the words you have selected, fill in the blank spaces in the story.

Now you've created your own hilarious MAD LIBS® game!

AMAZON ALLIES

FIRST NAME (FEMALE) _____

PLURAL NOUN _____

NUMBER _____

ADJECTIVE _____

PART OF THE BODY _____

VERB _____

OCCUPATION _____

ADJECTIVE _____

VERB _____

ADJECTIVE _____

NOUN _____

ADJECTIVE _____

ARTICLE OF CLOTHING _____

ADJECTIVE _____

PLURAL NOUN _____

NOUN _____

ANIMAL _____

MAD LIBS®

AMAZON ALLIES

Queen _____ is Wonder Woman's mother and leader of
FIRST NAME (FEMALE)

the _____. For over _____ centuries, she's led the
PLURAL NOUN   NUMBER

Amazons with a/an _____ heart and a firm _____.
ADJECTIVE   PART OF THE BODY

She considers it an honor to serve her people and will _____
VERB

them at any cost.

Philippus is a/an _____ and one of Hippolyta's most _____
OCCUPATION   ADJECTIVE

advisors. Her ability to _____ in the face of _____
VERB   ADJECTIVE

danger makes her a true hero.

General Antiope is Wonder Woman's _____. When the
NOUN

_____ princess was small, Antiope taught her how to use her
ADJECTIVE

_____ in battle.
ARTICLE OF CLOTHING

Artemis is a/an _____ warrior from a lost tribe of
ADJECTIVE

_____. She knows how to use a/an _____ with
PLURAL NOUN   NOUN

the fierceness of a/an _____.
ANIMAL

MAD LIBS® is fun to play with friends, but you can also play it by yourself! To begin with, DO NOT look at the story on the page below. Fill in the blanks on this page with the words called for. Then, using the words you have selected, fill in the blank spaces in the story.

Now you've created your own hilarious MAD LIBS® game!

THE GODS OF OLYMPUS

NOUN _____

NUMBER _____

PLURAL NOUN _____

ADJECTIVE _____

NOUN _____

OCCUPATION _____

NOUN _____

ADJECTIVE _____

A PLACE _____

VERB _____

ANIMAL _____

PART OF THE BODY (PLURAL) _____

MAD☺LIBS®

THE GODS OF OLYMPUS

1. Zeus is the _____ of the Gods. In his time, he's fathered
    <u>NOUN</u>

    over _____ offspring. Which of these _____ is
    <u>NUMBER</u>   <u>PLURAL NOUN</u>

    not his child?

    (a) Ares, (b) Eris, (c) Apollo, (d) Hera

2. Athena is very _____. She can soothe almost anyone with
    <u>ADJECTIVE</u>

    her _____. That's why she's the _____ of what?
    <u>NOUN</u>   <u>OCCUPATION</u>

    (a) Love, (b) Wisdom, (c) the Sun, (d) Mystery

3. This _____ is Zeus's daughter. She spreads _____
    <u>NOUN</u>   <u>ADJECTIVE</u>

    love to people all over (the) _____. Who is she?
    <u>A PLACE</u>

    (a) Hestia, (b) Hermes, (c) Aphrodite, (d) Hades

4. Ares only wants to _____. He's ferocious like a/an
    <u>VERB</u>

    _____ and thirsts for the _____ of his
    <u>ANIMAL</u>   <u>PART OF THE BODY (PLURAL)</u>

    enemies. What is he the God of?

    (a) War, (b) Night, (c) Darkness, (d) Evil

ANSWERS: 1. (d) 2. (b) 3. (c) 4. (a)

From WONDER WOMAN™ MAD LIBS® • ™ & © DC Comics. (s18)
Published in 2018 by Mad Libs, an imprint of Penguin Random House LLC.

MAD LIBS® is fun to play with friends, but you can also play it by yourself! To begin with, DO NOT look at the story on the page below. Fill in the blanks on this page with the words called for. Then, using the words you have selected, fill in the blank spaces in the story.

Now you've created your own hilarious MAD LIBS® game!

A WARRIOR TRAINS

NOUN _____

ANIMAL (PLURAL) _____

FIRST NAME (FEMALE) _____

A PLACE _____

OCCUPATION _____

VERB ENDING IN "ING" _____

NOUN _____

ADJECTIVE _____

PART OF THE BODY _____

VERB ENDING IN "ING" _____

ARTICLE OF CLOTHING _____

NOUN _____

NUMBER _____

PLURAL NOUN _____

NOUN _____

MAD LIBS®

A WARRIOR TRAINS

The _____ rose and the _____ cried out. It was
        NOUN   ANIMAL (PLURAL)

morning on Themyscira but _____ had been up for hours.
                            FIRST NAME (FEMALE)

Her aunt, General Antiope, was training her in (the) _____.
                                                      A PLACE

As the Amazons' resident _____, Antiope was good at
                            OCCUPATION

_____. She could throw a/an _____ and
VERB ENDING IN "ING"   NOUN

block a/an _____ kick to the _____. On this day,
            ADJECTIVE   PART OF THE BODY

she was _____ Diana to use her _____ to
        VERB ENDING IN "ING"   ARTICLE OF CLOTHING

defend herself. It wasn't as easy as it looked. The royal _____
                                                            NOUN

was good, but she had much to learn. After Diana skipped her lesson

one day, Antiope made her fight _____ _____ to
                                  NUMBER   PLURAL NOUN

teach her a lesson. *One day she will become the* _____, Antiope
                                                    NOUN

thought. *She must be ready.*

MAD LIBS® is fun to play with friends, but you can also play it by yourself! To begin with, DO NOT look at the story on the page below. Fill in the blanks on this page with the words called for. Then, using the words you have selected, fill in the blank spaces in the story.

Now you've created your own hilarious MAD LIBS® game!

GOODBYE, PARADISE

VERB _____

NOUN _____

ADJECTIVE _____

A PLACE _____

EXCLAMATION _____

OCCUPATION _____

ADJECTIVE _____

SILLY WORD _____

NOUN _____

PART OF THE BODY _____

PERSON IN ROOM _____

PLURAL NOUN _____

NOUN _____

ANIMAL _____

VERB _____

NOUN _____

ADJECTIVE _____

MAD LIBS®

GOODBYE, PARADISE

Hippolyta: The day has come for you to _____, Diana. I
VERB

stand before you a proud _____. Are you ready to embark on
NOUN

this _____ journey to (the) _____?
ADJECTIVE A PLACE

Diana: _____, Mother! I'm ready to become the
EXCLAMATION

_____ of peace in the outside world. I promise to do my
OCCUPATION

_____ duty and make you proud.
ADJECTIVE

Hippolyta: I'm already proud, my dear _____. From the
SILLY WORD

moment you came into my _____, you had my _____
NOUN PART OF THE BODY

in your hands.

Diana: I will miss you, _____, and all the other
PERSON IN ROOM

_____.
PLURAL NOUN

Hippolyta: We shall miss you as well. Remember to always be a/an

_____, Diana.
NOUN

Diana: It's like you've always said, "A/An _____ that can
ANIMAL

_____ will get the _____!"
VERB NOUN

Hippolyta: _____ luck, my daughter. You will be missed.
ADJECTIVE

From WONDER WOMAN™ MAD LIBS® • ™ & © DC Comics. (s18)
Published in 2018 by Mad Libs, an imprint of Penguin Random House LLC.

MAD LIBS® is fun to play with friends, but you can also play it by yourself! To begin with, DO NOT look at the story on the page below. Fill in the blanks on this page with the words called for. Then, using the words you have selected, fill in the blank spaces in the story.

Now you've created your own hilarious MAD LIBS® game!

THE OUTSIDE WORLD

A PLACE _____

PART OF THE BODY (PLURAL) _____

ADJECTIVE _____

PLURAL NOUN _____

PART OF THE BODY _____

VERB ENDING IN "ING" _____

A PLACE _____

ARTICLE OF CLOTHING _____

NOUN _____

VEHICLE _____

PART OF THE BODY _____

TYPE OF LIQUID _____

TYPE OF FOOD _____

ADJECTIVE _____

VERB _____

PLURAL NOUN _____

MAD LIBS®

THE OUTSIDE WORLD

When I arrived at (the) _____, I couldn't believe my
<small>A PLACE</small>

_____. There were so many _____ lights
<small>PART OF THE BODY (PLURAL)</small>   <small>ADJECTIVE</small>

and tall _____. It made my _____ ache. As I
<small>PLURAL NOUN</small>   <small>PART OF THE BODY</small>

began _____ through (the) _____, I noticed
<small>VERB ENDING IN "ING"</small>   <small>A PLACE</small>

people looking at my _____. I suppose it looked
<small>ARTICLE OF CLOTHING</small>

strange to see a/an _____ wearing such a thing. A man in a/an
<small>NOUN</small>

_____ almost ran over my _____. That was scary!
<small>VEHICLE</small>   <small>PART OF THE BODY</small>

Then a kind woman offered me a sip of _____ and a bite
<small>TYPE OF LIQUID</small>

of _____. It was _____! But I had to focus. I wasn't
<small>TYPE OF FOOD</small>   <small>ADJECTIVE</small>

there to _____ and gawk at _____ all day long. I
<small>VERB</small>   <small>PLURAL NOUN</small>

had a mission to fulfill.

MAD LIBS® is fun to play with friends, but you can also play it by yourself! To begin with, DO NOT look at the story on the page below. Fill in the blanks on this page with the words called for. Then, using the words you have selected, fill in the blank spaces in the story.

Now you've created your own hilarious MAD LIBS® game!

I AM WONDER WOMAN

EXCLAMATION _____

FIRST NAME (FEMALE) _____

A PLACE _____

ADJECTIVE _____

NOUN _____

NOUN _____

ADJECTIVE _____

NOUN _____

VERB _____

OCCUPATION _____

PLURAL NOUN _____

A PLACE _____

VERB ENDING IN "ING" _____

PLURAL NOUN _____

VERB _____

PART OF THE BODY _____

MAD LIBS®

I AM WONDER WOMAN

_____, citizens! I am _____ of (the) _____.
EXCLAMATION   FIRST NAME (FEMALE)   A PLACE

I've been sent to your _____ country by my _____.
                     ADJECTIVE   NOUN

I grew up on a/an _____, far away from this place. Do not
                     NOUN

think that makes me _____. I am still a/an _____.
                     ADJECTIVE   NOUN

I _____ just as you do. I am also a/an _____. That
   VERB   OCCUPATION

means I never give up, even when the _____ are stacked
                                PLURAL NOUN

against me. I come to (the) _____ with a message of hope. In
                       A PLACE

my life, I've learned that _____ together is the only
                  VERB ENDING IN "ING"

way forward, and I am prepared to help _____ at any cost.
                          PLURAL NOUN

I promise to always _____ for peace with my _____
                 VERB   PART OF THE BODY

held high. I am proud to be your Wonder Woman.

From WONDER WOMAN™ MAD LIBS® • ™ & © DC Comics. (s18)
Published in 2018 by Mad Libs, an imprint of Penguin Random House LLC.

MAD LIBS® is fun to play with friends, but you can also play it by yourself! To begin with, DO NOT look at the story on the page below. Fill in the blanks on this page with the words called for. Then, using the words you have selected, fill in the blank spaces in the story.

Now you've created your own hilarious MAD LIBS® game!

AMAZON IN ACTION

ADJECTIVE _____

EXCLAMATION _____

COLOR _____

TYPE OF LIQUID _____

A PLACE _____

NOUN _____

VERB (PAST TENSE) _____

NOUN _____

PART OF THE BODY (PLURAL) _____

ADJECTIVE _____

ARTICLE OF CLOTHING _____

PLURAL NOUN _____

NOUN _____

ADJECTIVE _____

NUMBER _____

PART OF THE BODY (PLURAL) _____

ADJECTIVE _____

MAD LIBS

AMAZON IN ACTION

This is Secret Agent Steve Trevor reporting on the _____
_____ADJECTIVE_____
incident with Wonder Woman. All I can say is _____! A
_____EXCLAMATION_____
group of crooks stole a container of _____ _____.
_____COLOR_____TYPE OF LIQUID
They were going to use it to destroy (the) _____. Not if
_____A PLACE_____
Wonder _____ had anything to say about it! She _____
_____NOUN_____VERB (PAST TENSE)
into action like a seasoned _____, tossing crooks by their
_____NOUN_____
_____. It was amazing. The _____ crooks
PART OF THE BODY (PLURAL)_____ADJECTIVE
fired their guns at her, but she held up her _____
_____ARTICLE OF CLOTHING
and the _____ bounced right off. Then she used her
_____PLURAL NOUN_____
_____ to make them tell the truth. One crook was so
_____NOUN_____
_____, he admitted to _____ other crimes! I thought
____ADJECTIVE_____NUMBER
my _____ must have been deceiving me. Take it
____PART OF THE BODY (PLURAL)
from me, Wonder Woman is a/an _____ hero.
_____ADJECTIVE

MAD LIBS® is fun to play with friends, but you can also play it by yourself! To begin with, DO NOT look at the story on the page below. Fill in the blanks on this page with the words called for. Then, using the words you have selected, fill in the blank spaces in the story.

Now you've created your own hilarious MAD LIBS® game!

GIFTS FROM THE GODS

ADJECTIVE _____

VERB _____

COLOR _____

CELEBRITY _____

NOUN _____

ADJECTIVE _____

PLURAL NOUN _____

NUMBER _____

PART OF THE BODY (PLURAL) _____

PLURAL NOUN _____

PERSON IN ROOM _____

ADJECTIVE _____

ADJECTIVE _____

SILLY WORD _____

PART OF THE BODY (PLURAL) _____

ADJECTIVE _____

ARTICLE OF CLOTHING _____

MAD LIBS®

GIFTS FROM THE GODS

Wonder Woman uses a handful of _____ items to _____
_{ADJECTIVE}   _{VERB}

against crime, like:

- The _____ Lasso of Truth that was given to her by
  _{COLOR}

  _____. It may look like a simple _____, but it
  _{CELEBRITY}   _{NOUN}

  has a very _____ feature: When _____ become
  _{ADJECTIVE}   _{PLURAL NOUN}

  tangled in it, they're forced to tell the truth.

- _____ metal gauntlets, which Wonder Woman wears on her
  _{NUMBER}

  _____ and uses to deflect _____.
  _{PART OF THE BODY (PLURAL)}   _{PLURAL NOUN}

  They were forged by _____ from a/an _____
  _{PERSON IN ROOM}   _{ADJECTIVE}

  metal.

- A/An _____ blade, known as the _____, that
  _{ADJECTIVE}   _{SILLY WORD}

  strikes fear in the _____ of her enemies. She uses
  _{PART OF THE BODY (PLURAL)}

  this along with her _____ shield, which attaches to the
  _{ADJECTIVE}

  back of her _____.
  _{ARTICLE OF CLOTHING}

MAD LIBS® is fun to play with friends, but you can also play it by yourself! To begin with, DO NOT look at the story on the page below. Fill in the blanks on this page with the words called for. Then, using the words you have selected, fill in the blank spaces in the story.

Now you've created your own hilarious MAD LIBS® game!

THE CHEETAH STRIKES

EXCLAMATION _____

A PLACE _____

COLOR _____

ADJECTIVE _____

OCCUPATION _____

FIRST NAME (FEMALE) _____

PLURAL NOUN _____

ADJECTIVE _____

ANIMAL _____

NOUN _____

ADJECTIVE _____

VERB ENDING IN "ING" _____

ADJECTIVE _____

PART OF THE BODY _____

A PLACE _____

MAD LIBS®

THE CHEETAH STRIKES

"_____!" Cheetah screeched. She was breaking into (the)
   EXCLAMATION

_____ when Wonder Woman caught her _____-handed.
  A PLACE   COLOR

Cheetah might seem _____, but she wasn't always a/an
                                   ADJECTIVE

_____. Before her life of crime, she was _____
 OCCUPATION   FIRST NAME (FEMALE)

Ann Minerva, an archaeologist and expert on ancient _____.
                                               PLURAL NOUN

Then a/an _____ curse turned her into a raging _____.
        ADJECTIVE   ANIMAL

Wonder Woman tried to save Cheetah, but it was no use. Her

_____ had already turned to the dark side. On this night, the
 NOUN

_____ Amazon raced to stop Cheetah from _____
 ADJECTIVE   VERB ENDING IN "ING"

more evil acts, but the villain wasn't going down without a fight. She

used her _____ _____ to scratch Wonder Woman,
      ADJECTIVE   PART OF THE BODY

stunning her briefly. This allowed Cheetah to escape through (the)

_____ and take off into the night!
 A PLACE

MAD LIBS® is fun to play with friends, but you can also play it by yourself! To begin with, DO NOT look at the story on the page below. Fill in the blanks on this page with the words called for. Then, using the words you have selected, fill in the blank spaces in the story.

Now you've created your own hilarious MAD LIBS® game!

WHICH DOCTOR

ADJECTIVE _____

TYPE OF LIQUID _____

TYPE OF LIQUID _____

ADJECTIVE _____

PLURAL NOUN _____

VERB _____

PART OF THE BODY _____

NOUN _____

A PLACE _____

A PLACE _____

NOUN _____

OCCUPATION _____

PLURAL NOUN _____

MAD LIBS®

WHICH DOCTOR

Wonder Woman has fought a few _____ doctors in her time.
_{ADJECTIVE}

Do you know which is which?

1. This doctor mixes _____ with _____ to
   TYPE OF LIQUID   TYPE OF LIQUID

   create _____ chemical _____, which she uses
   ADJECTIVE   PLURAL NOUN

   to _____ Wonder Woman.
   VERB

   (a) Doctor Evil, (b) Doctor Liquid, (c) Doctor Poison, (d) Doctor Mist

2. This doctor can control a person's _____ and make them
   PART OF THE BODY

   believe anything he chooses. He's a/an _____ that dreams
   NOUN

   of one day ruling (the) _____.
   A PLACE

   (a) Doctor Psycho, (b) Doctor Mindbreaker, (c) Doctor Brainz,

   (d) Doctor Mental

3. This doctor controls all of (the) _____. Each and every
   A PLACE

   _____ is at her disposal. As an expert _____,
   NOUN   OCCUPATION

   she can access your _____ and use them against you.
   PLURAL NOUN

   (a) Doctor Power, (b) Doctor Universe, (c) Doctor Fright,

   (d) Doctor Cyber

ANSWERS: 1. (c) 2. (a) 3. (d)

From WONDER WOMAN™ MAD LIBS® • ™ & © DC Comics. (s18)
Published in 2018 by Mad Libs, an imprint of Penguin Random House LLC.

MAD LIBS® is fun to play with friends, but you can also play it by yourself! To begin with, DO NOT look at the story on the page below. Fill in the blanks on this page with the words called for. Then, using the words you have selected, fill in the blank spaces in the story.

Now you've created your own hilarious MAD LIBS® game!

UNDERCOVER

A PLACE _____

COLOR _____

ARTICLE OF CLOTHING _____

COLOR _____

FIRST NAME (FEMALE) _____

VERB ENDING IN "ING" _____

ANIMAL _____

PLURAL NOUN _____

NUMBER _____

A PLACE _____

ADJECTIVE _____

ADJECTIVE _____

TYPE OF LIQUID _____

ADVERB _____

NOUN _____

COLOR _____

ADJECTIVE _____

MAD LIBS®

UNDERCOVER

Night had fallen in (the) _____ and it was time to get to work.

A PLACE

When Wonder Woman's _____ _____ drew

COLOR · ARTICLE OF CLOTHING

too much attention, she donned an all-_____ suit and became

COLOR

Special Agent _____ Prince. She'd been _____

FIRST NAME (FEMALE) · VERB ENDING IN "ING"

an evil organization known as the _____'s _____

ANIMAL · PLURAL NOUN

for over _____ months. They had been kidnapping children and

NUMBER

keeping them in (the) _____. After searching the city, Agent

A PLACE

Prince had finally discovered their location: a/an _____

ADJECTIVE

warehouse downtown. She snuck past the _____ guard and

ADJECTIVE

slipped into the facility. There was _____ everywhere.

TYPE OF LIQUID

Someone knew she was coming. She _____ rushed the children to

ADVERB

safety and, once they were far away from danger, the building exploded

into a/an _____ of _____ fire. *It's a/an* _____

NOUN · COLOR · ADJECTIVE

thing I arrived when I did, thought Agent Prince.

From WONDER WOMAN™ MAD LIBS® • ™ & © DC Comics. (s18)
Published in 2018 by Mad Libs, an imprint of Penguin Random House LLC.

MAD LIBS® is fun to play with friends, but you can also play it by yourself! To begin with, DO NOT look at the story on the page below. Fill in the blanks on this page with the words called for. Then, using the words you have selected, fill in the blank spaces in the story.

Now you've created your own hilarious MAD LIBS® game!

A NIGHT OUT

FIRST NAME _____

ADJECTIVE _____

TYPE OF FOOD _____

TYPE OF LIQUID _____

ADJECTIVE _____

COLOR _____

VERB ENDING IN "ING" _____

CELEBRITY _____

VERB _____

PERSON IN ROOM _____

ANIMAL _____

A PLACE _____

NOUN _____

ADJECTIVE _____

MAD LIBS®

A NIGHT OUT

Steve Trevor: Hello, Wonder Woman. Thanks for inviting me to

_____'s Ristorante. I'm glad we can take a break and have
   FIRST NAME

a/an _____ dinner for once. I heard this place has great
   ADJECTIVE

_____. Let's order a bottle of _____.
TYPE OF FOOD   TYPE OF LIQUID

Wonder Woman: That sounds like a/an _____ idea. Steve,
                                      ADJECTIVE

you're turning _____. Is everything okay?
            COLOR

Steve Trevor: It's strange. Everyone is _____ at us. This
                             VERB ENDING IN "ING"

must be what it feels like to eat with _____.
                                  CELEBRITY

Wonder Woman: I wish they wouldn't _____. I'm a regular
                                     VERB

person, just like _____. I don't want special attention.
           PERSON IN ROOM

[*CRASH!*]

Steve Trevor: Uh-oh. The _____ is breaking into (the)
                       ANIMAL

_____ across the street. Grab your _____. There
A PLACE   NOUN

goes our _____ night out!
        ADJECTIVE

MAD LIBS® is fun to play with friends, but you can also play it by yourself! To begin with, DO NOT look at the story on the page below. Fill in the blanks on this page with the words called for. Then, using the words you have selected, fill in the blank spaces in the story.

Now you've created your own hilarious MAD LIBS® game!

MISSING IN ACTION

OCCUPATION _____

NUMBER _____

VERB _____

ADJECTIVE _____

A PLACE _____

ANIMAL (PLURAL) _____

PART OF THE BODY (PLURAL) _____

PLURAL NOUN _____

ADJECTIVE _____

ARTICLE OF CLOTHING _____

A PLACE _____

TYPE OF LIQUID _____

ADJECTIVE _____

COLOR _____

NOUN _____

ADJECTIVE _____

PLURAL NOUN _____

MAD LIBS®

MISSING IN ACTION

For those of you who don't know me, I'm Agent Etta Candy. I've been

a/an _____ for over _____ years. Trust me when I
     OCCUPATION   NUMBER

_____. I know my stuff. Our mission today is _____—
   VERB   ADJECTIVE

find Wonder Woman. She was last seen in (the) _____ fighting a
                              A PLACE

group of wild _____. They had huge _____
     ANIMAL (PLURAL)   PART OF THE BODY (PLURAL)

and sharp teeth. We believe the poor _____ were subject to
                          PLURAL NOUN

a/an _____ experiment. Wonder Woman's _____
   ADJECTIVE   ARTICLE OF CLOTHING

was found discarded near (the) _____. There were traces of
                        A PLACE

_____ on it, along with a/an _____ _____
 TYPE OF LIQUID   ADJECTIVE   COLOR

dust. We suspect Doctor _____ is involved. This is a highly
                    NOUN

_____ situation and we must be careful. Grab your
  ADJECTIVE

_____, and let's find our friend!
  PLURAL NOUN

From WONDER WOMAN™ MAD LIBS® • ™ & © DC Comics. (s18)
Published in 2018 by Mad Libs, an imprint of Penguin Random House LLC.

MAD LIBS® is fun to play with friends, but you can also play it by yourself! To begin with, DO NOT look at the story on the page below. Fill in the blanks on this page with the words called for. Then, using the words you have selected, fill in the blank spaces in the story.

Now you've created your own hilarious MAD LIBS® game!

CHALLENGER

EXCLAMATION _____

A PLACE _____

VERB ENDING IN "ING" _____

ADJECTIVE _____

NOUN _____

OCCUPATION _____

VERB _____

TYPE OF LIQUID _____

ARTICLE OF CLOTHING _____

VERB ENDING IN "S" _____

TYPE OF FOOD _____

PERSON IN ROOM _____

TYPE OF FOOD _____

VERB ENDING IN "ING" _____

Artemis: _____, Diana! The people of (the) _____

EXCLAMATION   A PLACE

may call you Wonder Woman, but not I. You spend so much time

_____ in the outside world that you've forgotten

VERB ENDING IN "ING"

about your _____ sisters. What does your _____

                  ADJECTIVE   NOUN

think, I wonder?

Wonder Woman: I am a/an _____ and I _____

                              OCCUPATION   VERB

proudly. You've had too much _____ today, Artemis. Calm

                            TYPE OF LIQUID

yourself.

Artemis: Put your _____ on and fight me. I'll show

                   ARTICLE OF CLOTHING

you what a true Wonder Woman _____ like!

                            VERB ENDING IN "S"

Wonder Woman: We are sisters. Let us enjoy some _____

                                                TYPE OF FOOD

instead. We'll share it with _____ and discuss what angers

                          PERSON IN ROOM

you.

Artemis: I do enjoy _____. Very well. There will be no

                     TYPE OF FOOD

_____ today.

VERB ENDING IN "ING"

MAD LIBS® is fun to play with friends, but you can also play it by yourself! To begin with, DO NOT look at the story on the page below. Fill in the blanks on this page with the words called for. Then, using the words you have selected, fill in the blank spaces in the story.

Now you've created your own hilarious MAD LIBS® game!

CIRCE

A PLACE _____

COLOR _____

TYPE OF LIQUID _____

OCCUPATION _____

NOUN _____

CELEBRITY _____

PART OF THE BODY _____

ANIMAL (PLURAL) _____

VERB (PAST TENSE) _____

PART OF THE BODY _____

COLOR _____

NOUN _____

ADJECTIVE _____

VERB _____

MAD LIBS

CIRCE

Wonder Woman entered (the) ＿＿＿＿＿＿ to find a bubbling
                                A PLACE

cauldron filled with ＿＿＿＿＿＿ ＿＿＿＿＿＿＿. Circe, the
                     COLOR   TYPE OF LIQUID

＿＿＿＿＿＿, was close by. Suddenly a/an ＿＿＿＿＿＿ began to
OCCUPATION   NOUN

fall toward Wonder Woman. She caught it with ease. "Fight me, Circe!"

Wonder Woman cried out. Circe emerged from the darkness like

＿＿＿＿＿＿ walking onto a stage. Her ＿＿＿＿＿＿ crackled
CELEBRITY   PART OF THE BODY

with magical energy. "I turn men into ＿＿＿＿＿＿, you know.
                               ANIMAL (PLURAL)

I'm happy to do the same to you," Circe said. She ＿＿＿＿＿＿ in
                                VERB (PAST TENSE)

Wonder Woman's direction but missed by an inch. Suddenly, Circe's

＿＿＿＿＿＿ began to glow bright ＿＿＿＿＿＿ as she conjured a
PART OF THE BODY   COLOR

giant ＿＿＿＿＿＿ out of thin air. "What do you think? It's not too
      NOUN

＿＿＿＿＿＿, is it?" she asked. "＿＿＿＿＿＿ for your destruction,
ADJECTIVE   VERB

Amazon." "Do your worst," growled Wonder Woman.

MAD LIBS® is fun to play with friends, but you can also play it by yourself! To begin with, DO NOT look at the story on the page below. Fill in the blanks on this page with the words called for. Then, using the words you have selected, fill in the blank spaces in the story.

Now you've created your own hilarious MAD LIBS® game!

INSPIRATION

PART OF THE BODY _____

PERSON IN ROOM (MALE) _____

TYPE OF FOOD _____

NOUN _____

ARTICLE OF CLOTHING _____

NOUN _____

ADJECTIVE _____

NOUN _____

PLURAL NOUN _____

ADJECTIVE _____

VERB ENDING IN "ING" _____

ADJECTIVE _____

EXCLAMATION _____

ADJECTIVE _____

MAD LIBS

INSPIRATION

Wonder Woman: Hello, Andy. I can tell from your _____

PART OF THE BODY

that you're upset about something. What's troubling you?

Andy: _____ has been giving me a hard time at school.

PERSON IN ROOM (MALE)

He threw _____ at me during lunch one day and then put

TYPE OF FOOD

a/an _____ in my _____.

NOUN — ARTICLE OF CLOTHING

Wonder Woman: That's no way to behave. Why would this

_____ do such things?

NOUN

Andy: He thinks I'm _____ because I don't play

ADJECTIVE

_____-ball like the rest of the _____ at recess.

NOUN — PLURAL NOUN

Wonder Woman: I have a/an _____ idea. I'll take you

ADJECTIVE

_____. We'll fly high into the sky and forget all about

VERB ENDING IN "ING"

that _____ bully for today. Would you like that?

ADJECTIVE

Andy: _____! You bet I would. You sure are _____,

EXCLAMATION — ADJECTIVE

Wonder Woman.

MAD LIBS® is fun to play with friends, but you can also play it by yourself! To begin with, DO NOT look at the story on the page below. Fill in the blanks on this page with the words called for. Then, using the words you have selected, fill in the blank spaces in the story.

Now you've created your own hilarious MAD LIBS® game!

ENEMIES LIST

ADJECTIVE _____

NUMBER _____

PART OF THE BODY _____

VERB _____

NOUN _____

OCCUPATION _____

NOUN _____

ADJECTIVE _____

NOUN _____

PART OF THE BODY (PLURAL) _____

ARTICLE OF CLOTHING _____

COLOR _____

OCCUPATION _____

PLURAL NOUN _____

NOUN _____

VERB _____

MAD LIBS®

ENEMIES LIST

Wonder Woman has a/an _____ Rogues Gallery of enemies
                          ADJECTIVE

who won't rest till she's defeated!

- **Giganta** can grow _____ stories high. She's fond of using her
                          NUMBER

  enormous _____ to _____ her enemies. Be
            PART OF THE BODY   VERB

  careful or she'll squish you like a/an _____!
                                              NOUN

- **Veronica Cale** is a/an _____ who uses her power and
                              OCCUPATION

  _____ to destroy Wonder Woman's reputation. Though
   NOUN

  she has a/an _____ mind, Cale only uses it for evil.
                ADJECTIVE

- **Silver Swan's** sonic _____ is deafening. One blast can
                            NOUN

  make your _____ hurt for days. She wears a/an
             PART OF THE BODY (PLURAL)

  _____ made of metal with _____ wings
   ARTICLE OF CLOTHING   COLOR

  she uses to fly.

- **Angle Man** is a master _____ known for stealing
                              OCCUPATION

  _____. His _____ of choice is a triangular
   PLURAL NOUN   NOUN

  device which helps him _____ through time and space.
                              VERB

MAD LIBS® is fun to play with friends, but you can also play it by yourself! To begin with, DO NOT look at the story on the page below. Fill in the blanks on this page with the words called for. Then, using the words you have selected, fill in the blank spaces in the story.

Now you've created your own hilarious MAD LIBS® game!

PEP TALK

ADJECTIVE _____

PLURAL NOUN _____

A PLACE _____

ANIMAL _____

CELEBRITY _____

NOUN _____

ADJECTIVE _____

FIRST NAME _____

NOUN _____

ADJECTIVE _____

NOUN _____

ADJECTIVE _____

PLURAL NOUN _____

ADJECTIVE _____

PEP TALK

What a/an _____ day I've had! First, I stopped the _____
ADJECTIVE   PLURAL NOUN

of (the) _____ from stealing a rare _____ from the
A PLACE   ANIMAL

zoo. Then I saved _____ from a falling _____. After
CELEBRITY   NOUN

that, something _____ happened. Someone started a fire at
ADJECTIVE

_____'s Wharf downtown, and I arrived too late to stop
FIRST NAME

it. The whole _____ burned to the ground. Thankfully no
NOUN

one got hurt. I'm trying the best I can, but sometimes it's _____
ADJECTIVE

to be a hero. My _____ told me I'd have _____ days
NOUN   ADJECTIVE

and that I shouldn't give up even when the _____ get tough. It
PLURAL NOUN

was some of the most _____ advice I've ever gotten. Here's to
ADJECTIVE

a brighter tomorrow!

MAD LIBS® is fun to play with friends, but you can also play it by yourself! To begin with, DO NOT look at the story on the page below. Fill in the blanks on this page with the words called for. Then, using the words you have selected, fill in the blank spaces in the story.

Now you've created your own hilarious MAD LIBS® game!

WAR ARRIVES

VERB _____

VERB _____

NOUN _____

NOUN _____

NOUN _____

ADJECTIVE _____

NOUN _____

ARTICLE OF CLOTHING _____

TYPE OF LIQUID _____

VERB _____

VERB ENDING IN "ING" _____

FIRST NAME (FEMALE) _____

PLURAL NOUN _____

NOUN _____

MAD LIBS®

WAR ARRIVES

Ares: At last we _____, Wonder Woman. _____ out
VERB   VERB

of my way or suffer my wrath.

Wonder Woman: You do not frighten me, _____ of War. My
NOUN

_____ told me all about you. I've been preparing for this day
NOUN

since I was just a little _____.
NOUN

Ares: _____ girl, do you think your golden _____
ADJECTIVE   NOUN

frightens me? You cannot stop a god with a/an _____.
ARTICLE OF CLOTHING

It's over, Diana. I will drain this world of _____ then watch
TYPE OF LIQUID

it _____!
VERB

Wonder Woman: You forget who you are _____ with,
VERB ENDING IN "ING"

Ares. I am _____, Princess of the _____.
FIRST NAME (FEMALE)   PLURAL NOUN

Though I seek peaceful solutions, I refuse to let a bully like you destroy

the world I've sworn to protect. Prepare for battle, you _____!
NOUN

From WONDER WOMAN™ MAD LIBS® • ™ & © DC Comics. (s18)
Published in 2018 by Mad Libs, an imprint of Penguin Random House LLC.